PLASTIC CANVAS

Window Accents & More™

By Alida Macor

The Needlecraft Shop • Berne, IN 46711 • NeedlecraftShop.com • **Window Accents & More** 1

Butterflies & Beads Valance

Size: Individual panel: 5⅛ inches W x 10⅛ inches H (13cm x 26cm)
Valance as shown (seven panels): 35 inches W x 10⅛ inches H (88.9cm x 26cm)
Skill Level: Beginner

Materials

- 3½ sheets 7-count plastic canvas
- Uniek Needloft plastic canvas yarn as listed in color key
- #3 pearl cotton as listed in color key
- 58 (5mm) pearl beads
- 8 brass clip-on curtain rings
- #16 tapestry needle
- Sewing needle and black thread

Project Notes

Yardage figures given in color key are for seven-panel valance shown in photo.

Weave yarn and pearl cotton ends neatly under stitches on reverse side of work so that they are not visible from front.

Stitching Step by Step

1 Cut seven panels from plastic canvas according to graphs (two from each sheet).

2 Stitch four yellow butterfly panels and three blue butterfly panels according to graphs. When other stitching is complete, Straight Stitch antennae using black #3 pearl cotton. (Background remains unstitched.)

3 Using sewing needle and black thread, stitch pearl beads to butterfly wings where indicated by red dots on graphs.

4 Lay out panels side by side, alternating blue and yellow butterflies, beginning and ending with yellow butterflies. Using white yarn throughout, Whipstitch panels together along straight side edges.

5 Overcast unfinished straight side edges on both ends of valance. Overcast top edge of valance. (Bottom scalloped edge is not Overcast.)

6 Attach clip-on curtain rings to top edge of valance at each end and at each seam between panels.

COLOR KEY

Yards	Plastic Canvas Yarn
21 (19.2m)	■ Black #00
8 (7.3m)	■ Tangerine #11
4 (3.7m)	☐ Lemon #20
7 (6.4m)	☐ Fern #23
4 (3.7m)	☐ Baby blue #36
38 (34.8m)	☐ White #41
7 (6.4m)	■ Yellow #57
11 (10.1m)	■ Bright blue #60
	╱ Black #00 Backstitch
	#3 Pearl Cotton
3 (2.7m)	╱ Black #310 Straight Stitch
	● Attach 5mm pearl bead

Color numbers given are for Uniek Needloft plastic canvas yarn and DMC #3 pearl cotton.

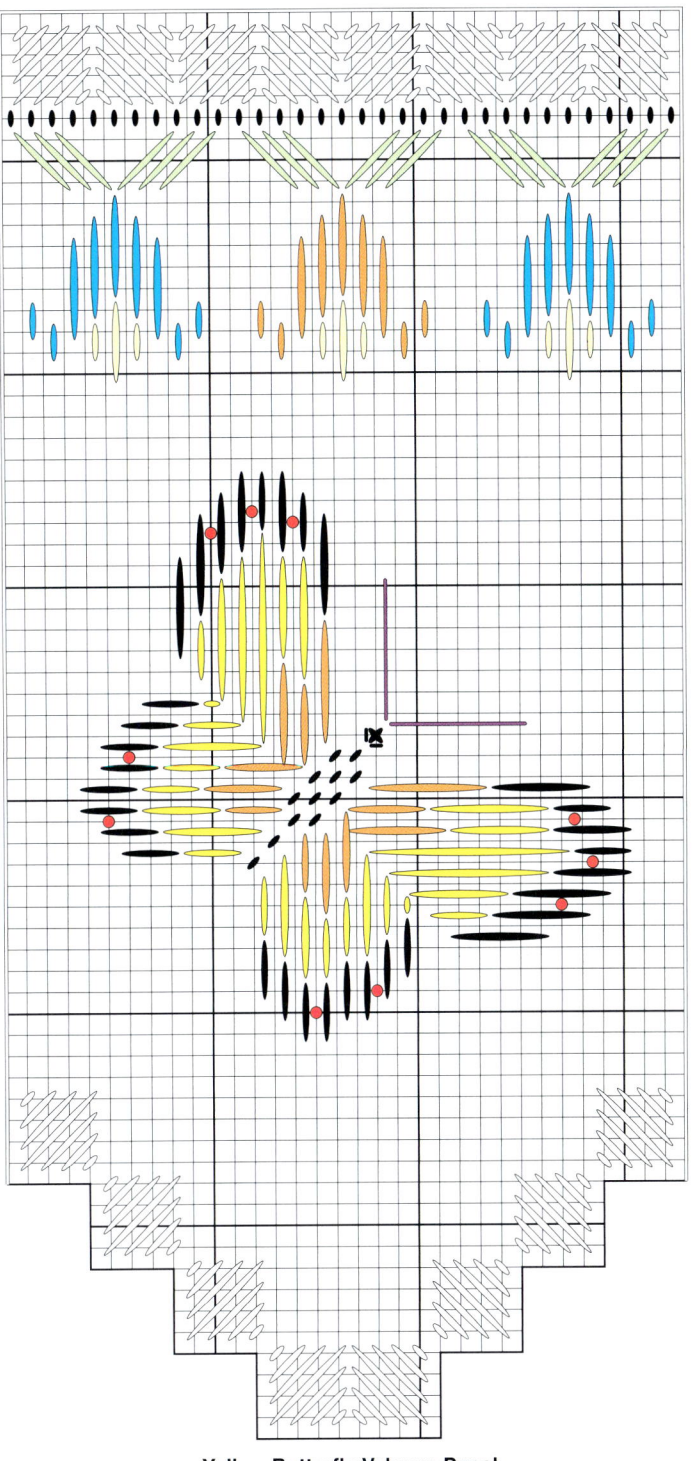

Yellow Butterfly Valance Panel
33 holes x 67 holes
Cut 4

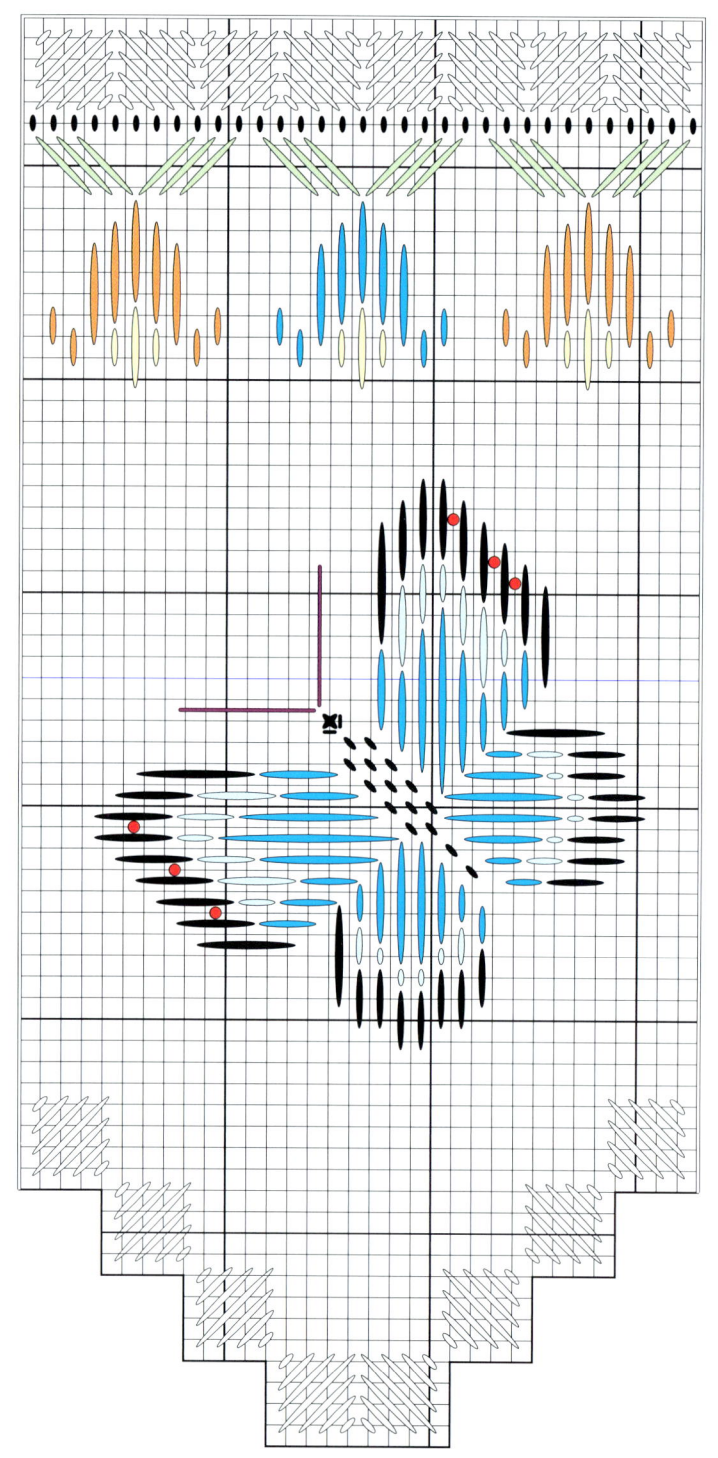

Blue Butterfly Valance Panel
33 holes x 67 holes
Cut 3

COLOR KEY	
Yards	**Plastic Canvas Yarn**
21 (19.2m)	■ Black #00
8 (7.3m)	■ Tangerine #11
4 (3.7m)	□ Lemon #20
7 (6.4m)	□ Fern #23
4 (3.7m)	□ Baby blue #36
38 (34.8m)	□ White #41
7 (6.4m)	□ Yellow #57
11 (10.1m)	■ Bright blue #60
	╱ Black #00 Backstitch
	#3 Pearl Cotton
3 (2.7m)	╱ Black #310 Straight Stitch
	● Attach 5mm pearl bead

Color numbers given are for Uniek Needloft plastic canvas yarn and DMC #3 pearl cotton.

4 Window Accents & More • *The Needlecraft Shop* • *Berne, IN 46711* • *NeedlecraftShop.com*

Butterflies & Beads Tiebacks

Size: 23½ inches W x 1½ inches H including white plastic rings (59.7cm x 3.8cm)

Skill Level: Beginner

Materials

- ¼ artist-size sheet 7-count plastic canvas
- Uniek Needloft plastic canvas yarn as listed in color key
- 4 (1-inch/2.5cm) white plastic rings
- #16 tapestry needle

Stitching Step by Step

1. Cut two tieback strips from plastic canvas according to graph, trimming ends identically.

2. Beginning at left end of strip, stitch each piece according to graph, continuing pattern and alternating tangerine and blue flowers across strip.

3. *Using white yarn throughout, Overcast edges of tieback strips:* Thread a 3-yard (2.7m) length of white yarn through center hole along one long edge; pull yarn ends even, centering yarn in hole. Working with one half of the yarn, Overcast straight edge, stitching through *every other hole* and working toward end. At tapered end of strip, stitch through *every hole,* Whipstitching a plastic ring at each end as you stitch.

4. Working in the same manner, Overcast all remaining unfinished edges, attaching plastic rings to both ends of tiebacks.

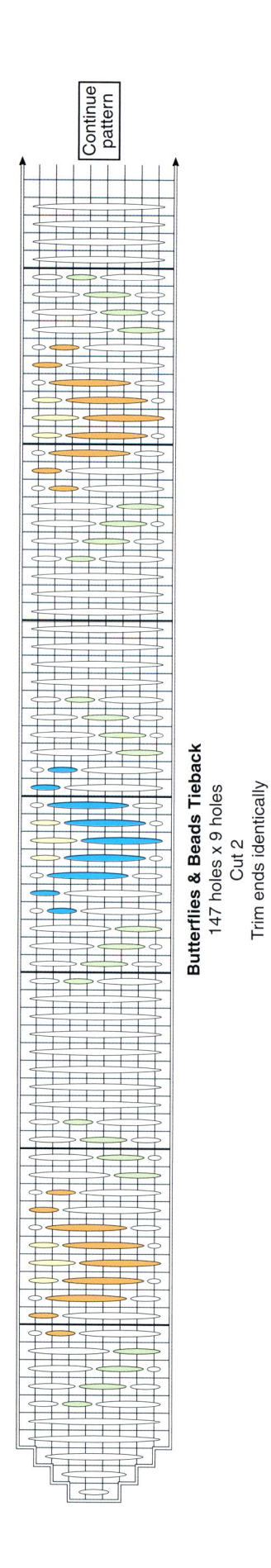

Butterflies & Beads Tieback
147 holes x 9 holes
Cut 2
Trim ends identically

Continue pattern

COLOR KEY

Yards	Plastic Canvas Yarn
3 (2.7m)	■ Tangerine #11
3 (2.7m)	□ Lemon #20
6 (5.5m)	■ Fern #23
24 (22m)	□ White #41
3 (2.7m)	■ Bright blue #60

Color numbers given are for Uniek Needloft plastic canvas yarn.

Butterflies & Beads Place Mat

Size: 16 inches W x 11 inches H (40.6cm x 27.9cm)
Skill Level: Beginner

Materials
- 1 sheet stiff 7-count plastic canvas
- Uniek Needloft plastic canvas yarn as listed in color key
- Worsted weight yarn as listed in color key
- #3 pearl cotton as listed in color key
- 10 (5mm) pearl beads
- #16 tapestry needle
- Sewing needle and black thread

Stitching Step by Step

1 Cut plastic canvas according to graph.

2 Using plastic canvas yarn according to graph, stitch border, flowers and butterfly.

3 Using white worsted weight yarn and referring to Fig. 1, fill in background with vertical rows of Half Cross Stitches, working in every other hole as shown, and beginning and ending yarn on reverse side of white border or other area of solid white stitching.

4 Straight Stitch butterfly antennae using black #3 pearl cotton.

5 Using sewing needle and black thread, stitch pearl beads to butterfly wings where indicated by red dots on graph.

6 Using white plastic canvas yarn, Overcast edges, stitching through *every other hole,* and working *two stitches* through each corner hole for complete coverage.

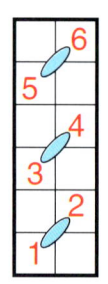

Fig. 1
Half Cross Stitches

COLOR KEY

Yards	Plastic Canvas Yarn
3 (2.7m)	■ Black #00
2 (1.8m)	■ Tangerine #11
3 (2.7m)	■ Fern #23
1 (0.9m)	■ Baby blue #36
24 (22m)	□ White #41
2 (1.8m)	■ Yellow #57
2 (1.8m)	■ Bright blue #60
	╱ Black #00 Backstitch
Worsted Weight Yarn	
38 (34.8m)	╱ White Half Cross Stitch
#3 Pearl Cotton	
	╱ Black #310 Straight Stitch
3 (2.7m)	● Attach 5mm pearl bead

Color numbers given are for Uniek Needloft plastic canvas yarn and DMC #3 pearl cotton.

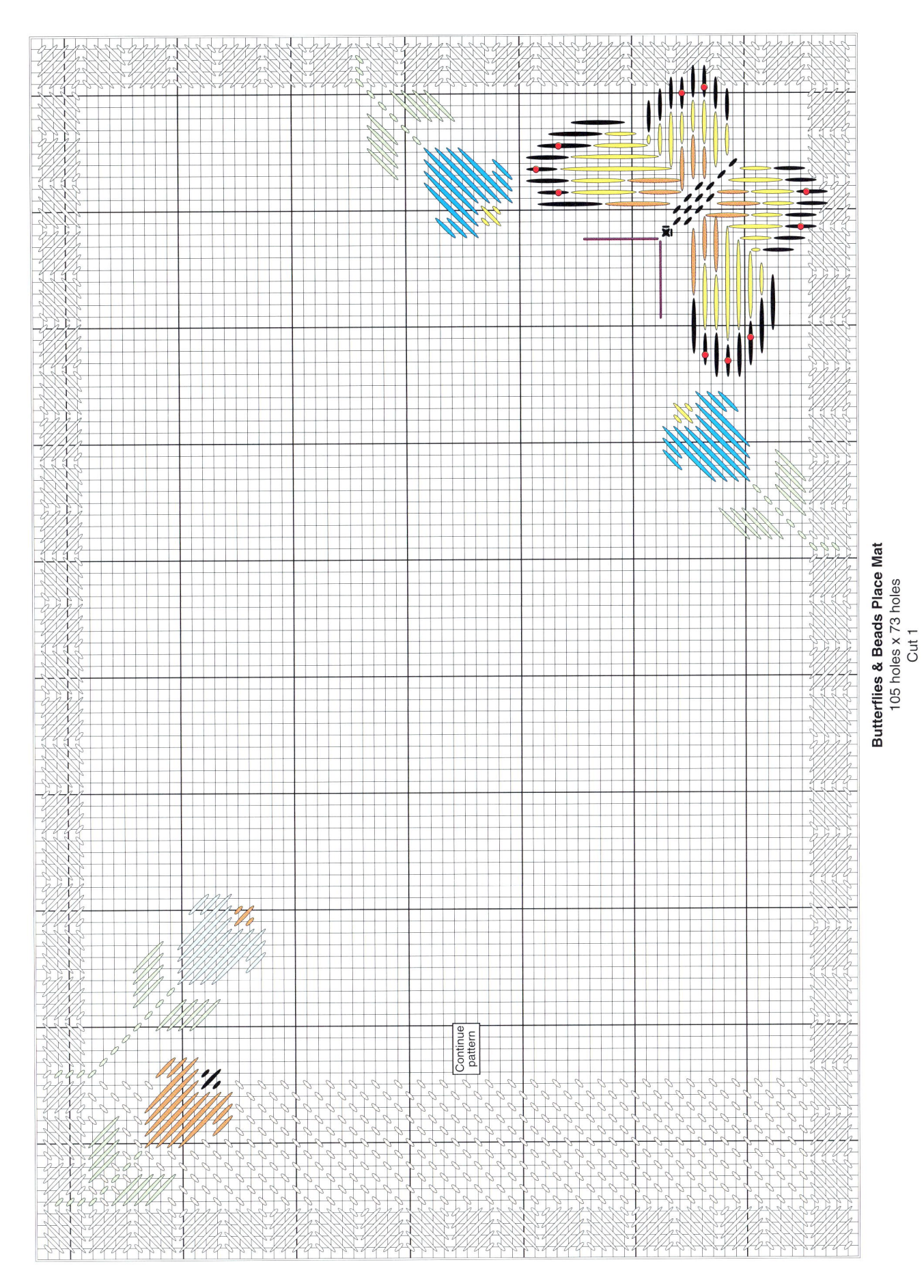

Butterflies & Beads Place Mat
105 holes x 73 holes
Cut 1

Flowerpot Garden Valance

Size: **Individual panel:** 4¾ inches W x 10½ inches H (12.1cm x 26.7cm)
Valance as shown (seven panels): 33 inches W x 10½ inches H (83.8cm x 26.7cm)
Skill Level: Beginner

Materials

- 3½ sheets clear 7-count plastic canvas
- Uniek Needloft plastic canvas yarn as listed in color key
- 7 (5mm) gold metallic beads
- 8 brass clip-on curtain rings
- #16 tapestry needle
- Sewing needle
- Sewing threads: light brown, light yellow

Project Notes

Yardage figures given in color key are for seven-panel valance shown in photo.

Weave yarn ends neatly under stitches on reverse side of work so that they are not visible from front.

Stitching Step by Step

1. Cut seven panels from plastic canvas according to graph (two from each sheet).

2. Stitch three panels according to graph. (Note that much of the background remains unstitched.) Stitch two panels substituting watermelon yarn for the yellow, and lemon yarn for the maple used to stitch the flower centers. Stitch one panel substituting tangerine yarn for the yellow, and lemon yarn for the maple flower center. Stitch the remaining panel substituting orchid yarn for the yellow, and lemon yarn for the maple flower center.

3. Straight Stitch flower stems using fern yarn. Backstitch outline below white edging at top using maple yarn. Using sewing needle and thread to match flower center, stitch a gold bead in the center of each flower, where indicated by red dot on graph.

4. Lay out panels side by side, in order according to flower color: yellow, watermelon, tangerine, yellow, orchid, watermelon, yellow. Using white yarn throughout, Whipstitch panels together along straight side edges.

5 Overcast unfinished straight side edges on both ends of valance. Overcast top edge of valance. (Bottom edge is not Overcast.)

6 Attach clip-on curtain rings to top edge of valance at each end and at each seam between panels.

COLOR KEY		
Yards		Plastic Canvas Yarn
3 (2.7m)		Tangerine #11
47 (43m)	■	Maple #13
3 (2.7m)		Lemon #20
14 (12.8m)	☐	Fern #23
21 (19.2m)	☐	White #41
3 (2.7m)		Orchid #44
6 (5.5m)		Watermelon #55
9 (8.2m)	☐	Yellow #57
	╱	Maple #13 Backstitch
	╱	Fern #23 Straight Stitch
	●	Attach 5mm gold bead

Color numbers given are for Uniek Needloft plastic canvas yarn.

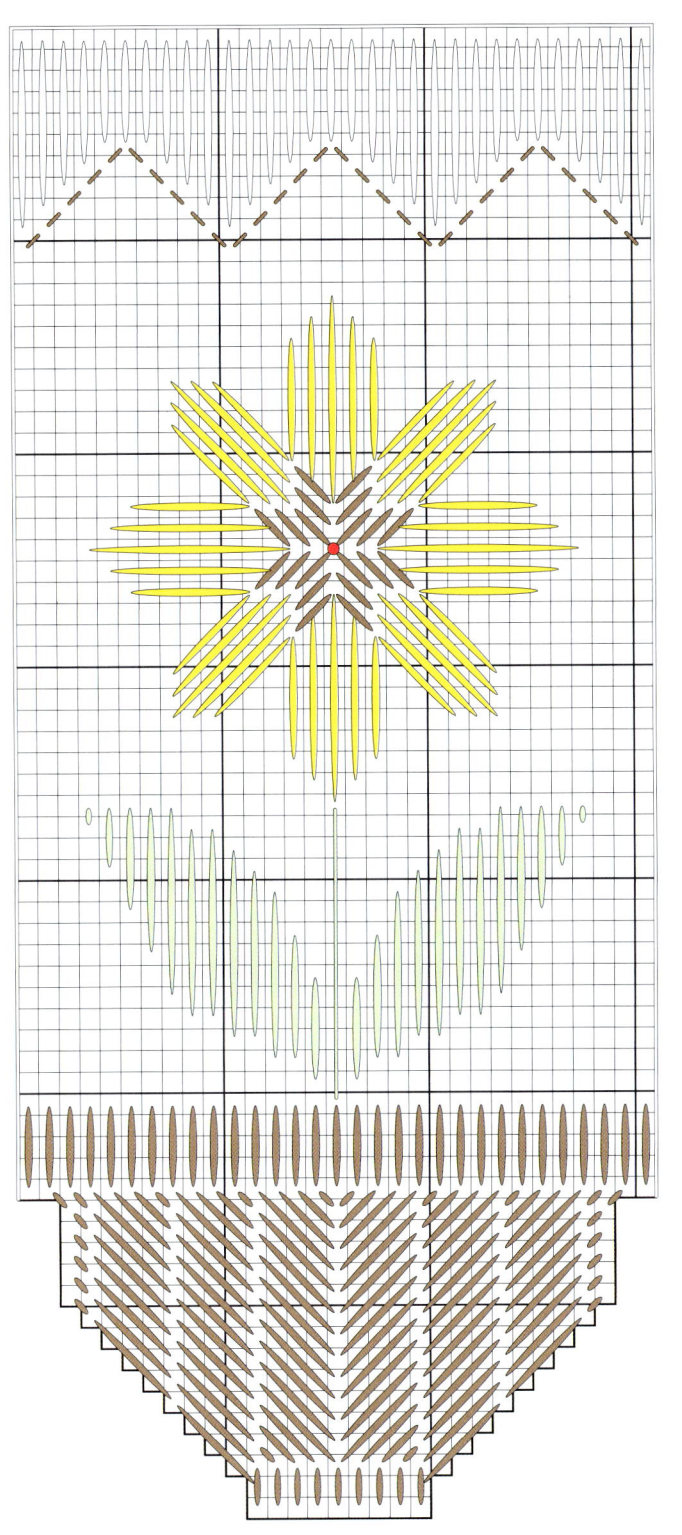

Flowerpot Garden Valance Panel
31 holes x 70 holes
Cut 7
Stitch 3 as shown
Stitch 2 substituting watermelon
for yellow and lemon for maple
flower center
Stitch 1 substituting tangerine
for yellow and lemon for maple
flower center
Stitch 1 substituting orchid for
yellow and lemon for maple
flower center

Flowerpot Garden Tiebacks

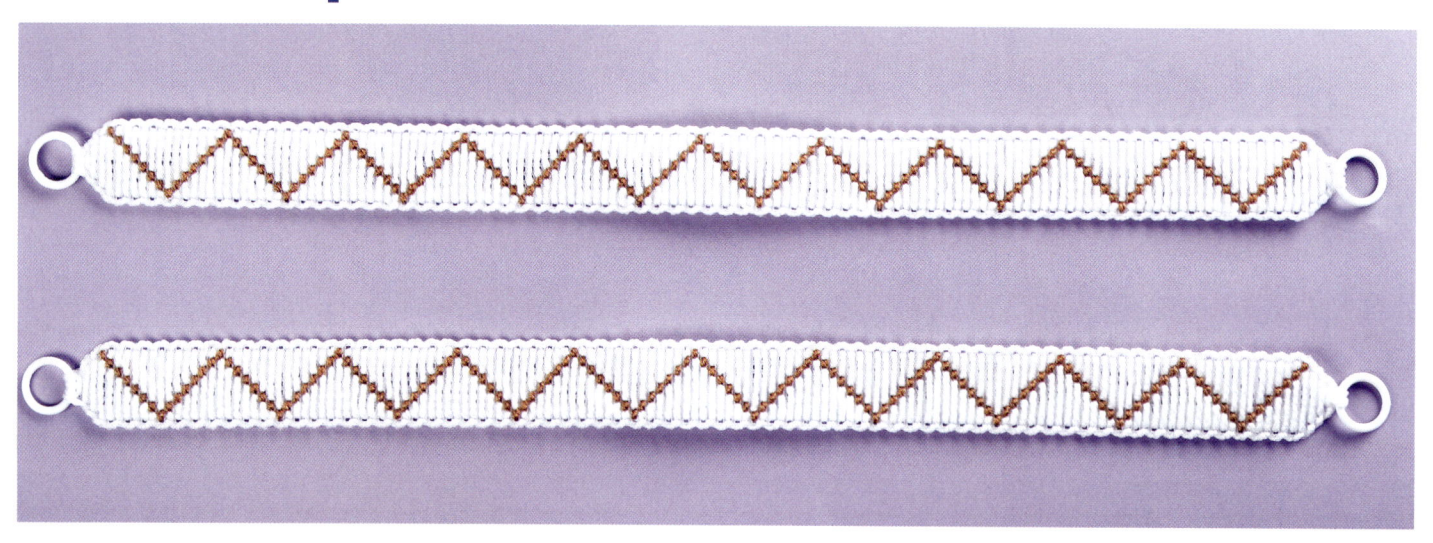

Size: 23½ inches W x 1½ inches H including white plastic rings (59.7cm x 3.8cm)
Skill Level: Beginner

Materials
- ¼ artist-size sheet 7-count plastic canvas
- Uniek Needloft plastic canvas yarn as listed in color key
- 4 (1-inch/2.5cm) white plastic rings
- #16 tapestry needle

Stitching Step by Step

1 Cut two tieback strips from plastic canvas according to graph, trimming ends identically.

2 Stitch each piece according to graph.

3 *Using white yarn throughout, Overcast edges of tieback strips:* Thread a 3-yard (2.7m) length of white yarn through center hole along one long edge; pull yarn ends even, centering yarn in hole. Working with one half of the yarn, Overcast edge, stitching through *every other hole* along straight edge and working toward end. At tapered end of strip, stitch through *every hole*, Whipstitching a plastic ring at each end as you stitch.

4 Working in the same manner, Overcast all remaining unfinished edges, attaching rings to both ends of tiebacks.

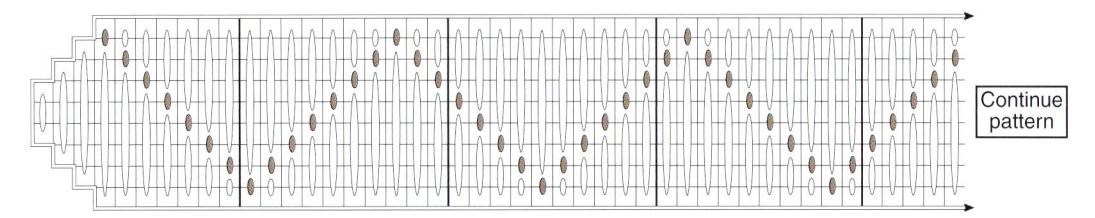

Flowerpot Garden Tieback
147 holes x 9 holes
Cut 2
Cut both ends identically

Continue pattern

COLOR KEY

Yards	Plastic Canvas Yarn
5 (4.6m)	■ Maple #13
26 (23.8m)	☐ White #41

Color numbers given are for Uniek Needloft plastic canvas yarn.

Flowerpot Garden Tissue Topper

14 **Window Accents & More** • The Needlecraft Shop • Berne, IN 46711 • NeedlecraftShop.com

Size: 4¾ inches W x 5⅝ inches H x 4¾ inches D (12.1cm x 14.3cm x 12.1cm); fits boutique-style box of tissues

Skill Level: Beginner

Materials

- 1½ sheets 7-count plastic canvas
- Uniek Needloft plastic canvas yarn as listed in color key
- 4 (5mm) gold metallic beads
- #16 tapestry needle
- Sewing needle
- Sewing threads: light brown, light yellow

Stitching Step by Step

1 Cut four side panels and one top from plastic canvas according to graphs.

2 Stitch top according to graph, Overcasting center opening with white yarn.

3 Stitch one side panel according to graph. On one of each of the remaining panels, substitute watermelon, tangerine and orchid yarn for the yellow yarn; substitute lemon yarn for the maple yarn used to stitch the flower centers. (Use maple yarn to stitch flowerpots on all sides.)

4 When background stitching is complete, Straight Stitch flower stems using fern yarn. Using sewing needle and thread to match flower center, stitch a gold bead in the center of each flower where indicated by red dot on graph.

5 Using maple yarn throughout, Whipstitch side panels together along side edges to form an open-ended square column. Whipstitch top to top edges of assembled sides.

6 Using white yarn, Overcast bottom edges of tissue topper.

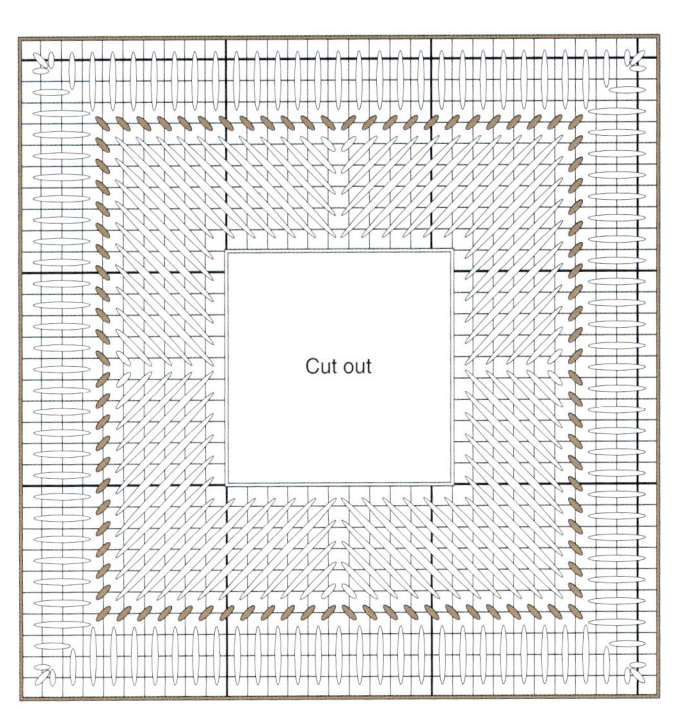

COLOR KEY

Yards	Plastic Canvas Yarn
3 (2.7m)	Tangerine #11
14 (12.8m)	■ Maple #13
1 (0.9m)	Lemon #20
5 (4.6m)	□ Fern #23
54 (49.4m)	□ White #41
3 (2.7m)	Orchid #44
3 (2.7m)	Watermelon #55
3 (2.7m)	□ Yellow #57
	╱ Fern #23 Straight Stitch
	● Attach 5mm gold bead

Color numbers given are for Uniek Needloft plastic canvas yarn.

Flowerpot Garden Tissue Topper Top
31 holes x 31 holes
Cut 1

Flowerpot Garden Tissue Topper Side
31 holes x 37 holes
Cut 4
Stitch 1 as shown
Stitch 1 each substituting watermelon,
tangerine and orchid for yellow,
and substituting lemon for
maple flower center

COLOR KEY	
Yards	**Plastic Canvas Yarn**
3 (2.7m)	Tangerine #11
14 (12.8m)	■ Maple #13
1 (0.9m)	Lemon #20
5 (4.6m)	☐ Fern #23
54 (49.4m)	☐ White #41
3 (2.7m)	Orchid #44
3 (2.7m)	Watermelon #55
3 (2.7m)	☐ Yellow #57
	∕ Fern #23 Straight Stitch
	● Attach 5mm gold bead

Color numbers given are for Uniek Needloft plastic canvas yarn.

Lucy Ladybug Magnet

Size: 2¼ inches W x 3¼ inches H
(5.7cm x 8.2cm)
Skill Level: Beginner

Materials

- 7-count plastic canvas:
    Small piece of clear soft
    Small piece of black
- Uniek Needloft plastic canvas yarn as listed in color key
- 2 (8mm) round wiggly eyes
- 1-inch (2.5cm) round self-adhesive magnet disk
- #16 tapestry needle
- Glue

Stitching Step by Step

1 Cut ladybug top from soft plastic canvas and ladybug bottom from black plastic canvas according to graphs.

2 Work all black stitches on top and bottom according to graphs.

3 Using watermelon yarn, work remaining stitches on ladybug top; as you stitch, Whipstitch together the facing edges indicated by arrows to give the ladybug dimension.

4 Using watermelon and black yarns according to graphs, Whipstitch ladybug top and bottom together.

5 Glue wiggly eyes to ladybug where indicated by red dots on graph; attach magnet to stitched area on bottom of ladybug.

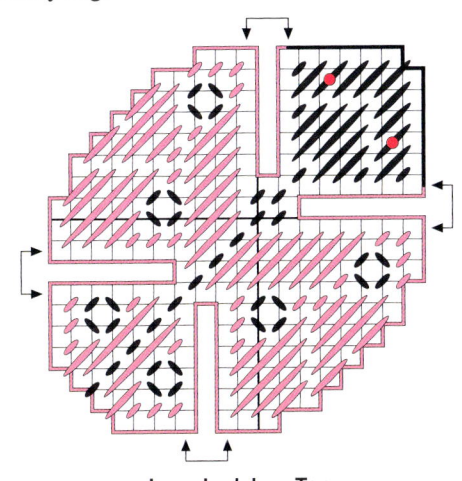

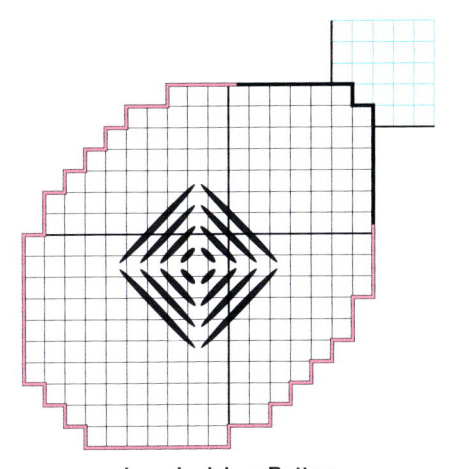

Lucy Ladybug Bottom
20 holes x 20 holes
Cut 1 from black plastic canvas,
cutting away blue lines

Lucy Ladybug Top
18 holes x 18 holes
Cut 1 from clear soft plastic canvas

COLOR KEY

Yards	Plastic Canvas Yarn
4 (3.7m)	■ Black #00
5 (4.6m)	■ Watermelon #55
	● Attach 8mm wiggly eye

Color numbers given are for Uniek Needloft plastic canvas yarn.

Flowerpot Garden Napkin Holder

Size: 17 inches W x 6¼ inches H x 2¼ inches D
(17.8cm x 15.8cm x 5.7cm)
Skill Level: Beginner

Materials
- 1 sheet stiff 7-count plastic canvas
- Uniek Needloft plastic canvas yarn as listed in color key
- Worsted weight yarn as listed in color key
- 2 ladybug buttons *or* beads
- #16 tapestry needle
- Sewing needle and white thread

Stitching Step by Step

1. Cut two pieces for front and back and two sides from plastic canvas according to graphs. Cut also one 45 x 14-hole piece for bottom; it will remain unstitched.

2. Stitch flowers *except stems* and white borders on front, back and sides according to graphs.

3. Using white worsted weight yarn and referring to Fig. 1 (page 8), fill in background with vertical rows of Half Cross Stitches, working in every other hole as shown, and beginning and ending yarn on reverse side of white border.

4. Straight Stitch flower stems using fern yarn. Using sewing needle and thread, stitch ladybug button or bead to front and back where indicated by red dot on graph.

5 Using white yarn throughout, Whipstitch sides to front and back, bottom edges even. Whipstitch unstitched base to bottom of assembled napkin holder. Overcast all remaining edges.

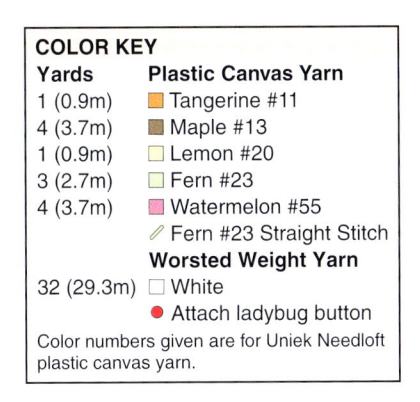

COLOR KEY

Yards	Plastic Canvas Yarn
1 (0.9m)	▨ Tangerine #11
4 (3.7m)	▨ Maple #13
1 (0.9m)	▨ Lemon #20
3 (2.7m)	▨ Fern #23
4 (3.7m)	▨ Watermelon #55
	╱ Fern #23 Straight Stitch
	Worsted Weight Yarn
32 (29.3m)	▢ White
	● Attach ladybug button

Color numbers given are for Uniek Needloft plastic canvas yarn.

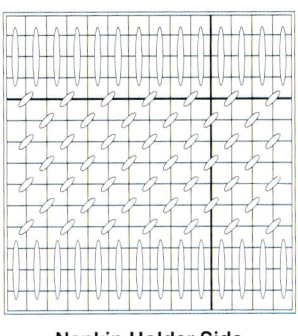

Napkin Holder Side
14 holes x 14 holes
Cut 2

Flowerpot Garden Napkin Holder
Front & Back
45 holes x 41 holes
Cut 2

Love Blooms Here

Size: 4 inches W x 6 inches H
(10.2cm x 15.2cm)
Skill Level: Beginner

Materials
- ½ sheet clear 10-count plastic canvas
- DMC 6-strand embroidery floss as listed in color key
- 4 x 6-inch (10.2cm x 15.2cm) white paper
- 4 x 6-inch (10.2cm x 15.2cm) frame
- #18 tapestry needle

Project Note
All stitches except flower stems are worked using all 6 strands of embroidery floss. Separate an 18-inch length of floss into individual strands. Recombine them without twisting; thread all 6 strands onto needle.

Stitching Step by Step

1. Cut plastic canvas according to graph.

2. Stitch flowers (except stems), lettering and butterflies according to graph.

3. Fill in uncoded background with white Continental Stitches.

4. Using 3 strands separated from a length of green floss, Straight Stitch flower stems.

5. Hold white paper behind stitched design; insert both pieces into frame.

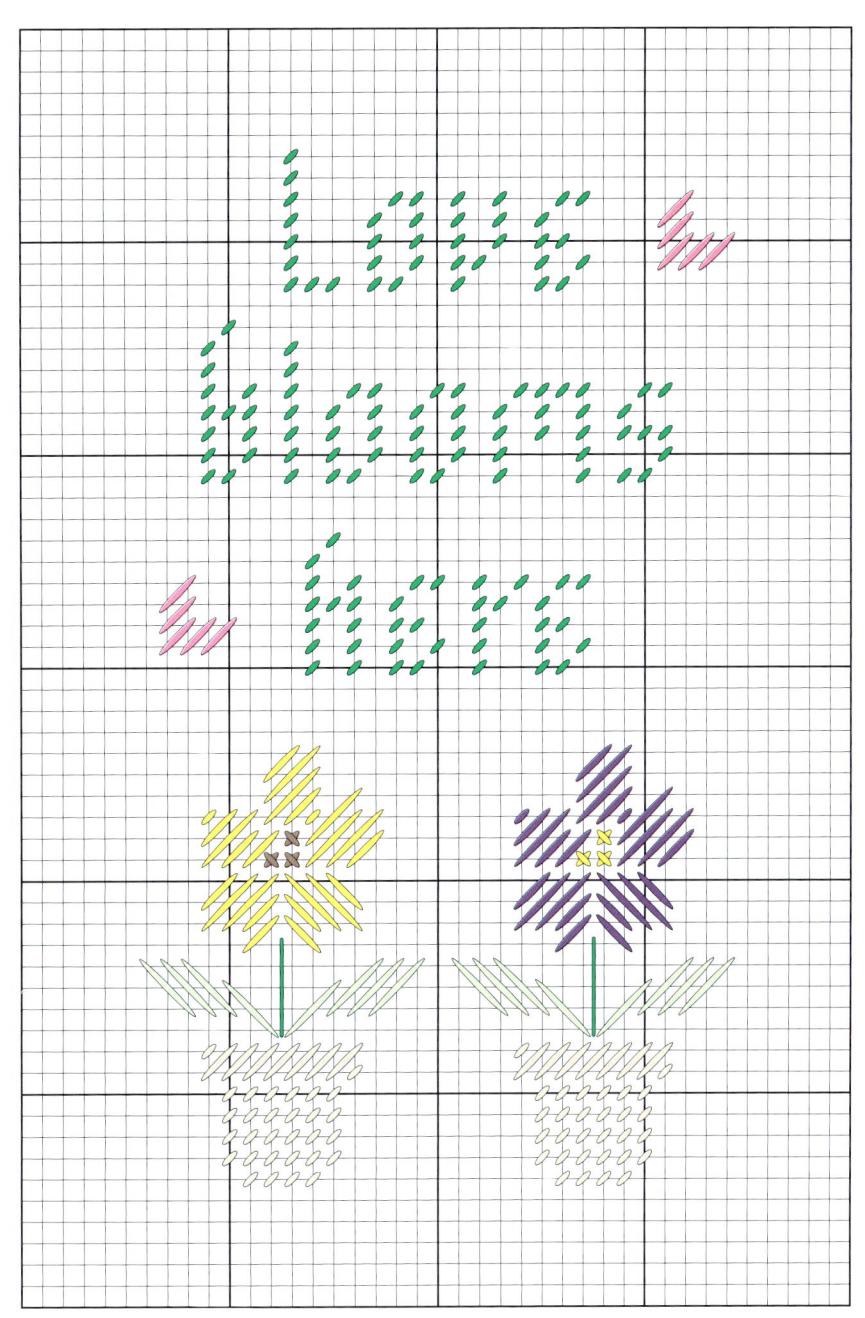

Love Blooms Here
40 holes x 60 holes
Cut 1

COLOR KEY	
Yards	**6-Strand Embroidery Floss**
1 (0.9m)	■ Purple #208
1 (0.9m)	■ Dark brown #433
2 (1.8m)	□ Medium brown #435
3 (2.7m)	■ Dark green #699
1 (0.9m)	□ Medium green #703
1 (0.9m)	□ Yellow #725
1 (0.9m)	■ Rose #3832
26 (23.8m)	Uncoded areas are White Continental Stitches
╱	Dark green #699 3-strand Straight Stitch

Color numbers given are for DMC 6-strand embroidery floss.

Woodland Birds Valance

Size: **Individual panel:** 5 inches W x 10½ inches H (12.7cm x 26.7cm)
Valance as shown (seven panels): 35 inches W x 10½ inches H (88.9cm x 26.7cm)
Skill Level: Beginner

Materials
- 3½ sheets 7-count plastic canvas
- Uniek Needloft plastic canvas yarn as listed in color key
- Worsted weight yarn as listed in color key
- Needloft metallic craft cord as listed in color key
- 7 (8mm) round wiggly eyes
- 8 brass clip-on curtain rings
- #16 tapestry needle
- Glue

Project Notes
Yardage figures given in color key are for seven-panel valance shown in photo.

Weave yarn and craft cord ends neatly under stitches on reverse side of work so that they are not visible from front.

Stitching Step by Step

1. Cut seven panels from plastic canvas according to graphs (two from each sheet).

2. Stitch four blue jay panels and three Baltimore oriole panels according to graphs.

3. When background stitching is complete, Straight Stitch beaks using black/silver craft cord; Straight Stitch bird legs and accents on blue jay wings and tail using black yarn. (Background remains unstitched.)

4. Glue wiggly eyes to birds where indicated by red dots on graphs.

5. Lay out panels side by side, alternating blue jays and orioles. Using white yarn throughout, Whipstitch panels together along straight side edges.

6. Overcast unfinished straight side edges on both ends of valance. Overcast top edge of valance. (Bottom edge is not Overcast.)

7. Attach clip-on curtain rings to top edge of valance at each end and at seams between panels.

COLOR KEY

Yards	Plastic Canvas Yarn
6 (5.5m)	☐ Tangerine #11
12 (11m)	☐ Maple #13
9 (8.2m)	☐ Fern #23
6 (5.5m)	☐ Christmas green #28
8 (7.3m)	☐ Royal #32
2 (1.8m)	☐ Sail blue #35
2 (1.8m)	☐ Silver #37
54 (49.4m)	☐ White #41
	Worsted Weight Yarn
17 (15.5m)	■ Black
	╱ Black Straight Stitch
	Metallic Craft Cord
2 (1.8m)	╱ Black/silver #55010 Straight Stitch
	● Attach 8mm wiggly eye

Color numbers given are for Uniek Needloft plastic canvas yarn and metallic craft cord.

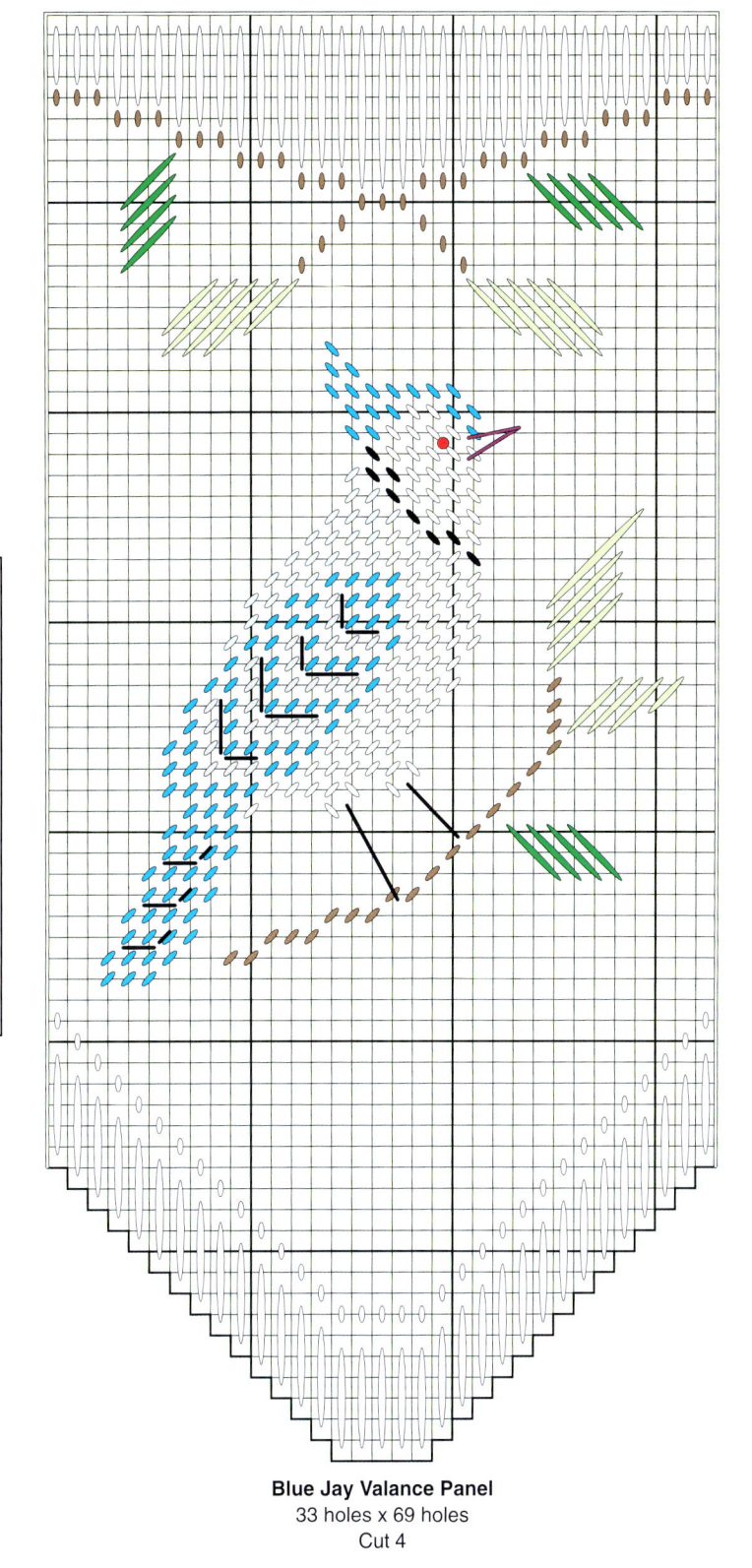

Blue Jay Valance Panel
33 holes x 69 holes
Cut 4

The Needlecraft Shop • Berne, IN 46711 • NeedlecraftShop.com • **Window Accents & More 23**

COLOR KEY

Yards	Plastic Canvas Yarn
6 (5.5m)	Tangerine #11
12 (11m)	Maple #13
9 (8.2m)	Fern #23
6 (5.5m)	Christmas green #28
8 (7.3m)	Royal #32
2 (1.8m)	Sail blue #35
2 (1.8m)	Silver #37
54 (49.4m)	White #41

Worsted Weight Yarn

17 (15.5m)	Black
	Black Straight Stitch

Metallic Craft Cord

2 (1.8m)	Black/silver #55010 Straight Stitch
●	Attach 8mm wiggly eye

Color numbers given are for Uniek Needloft plastic canvas yarn and metallic craft cord.

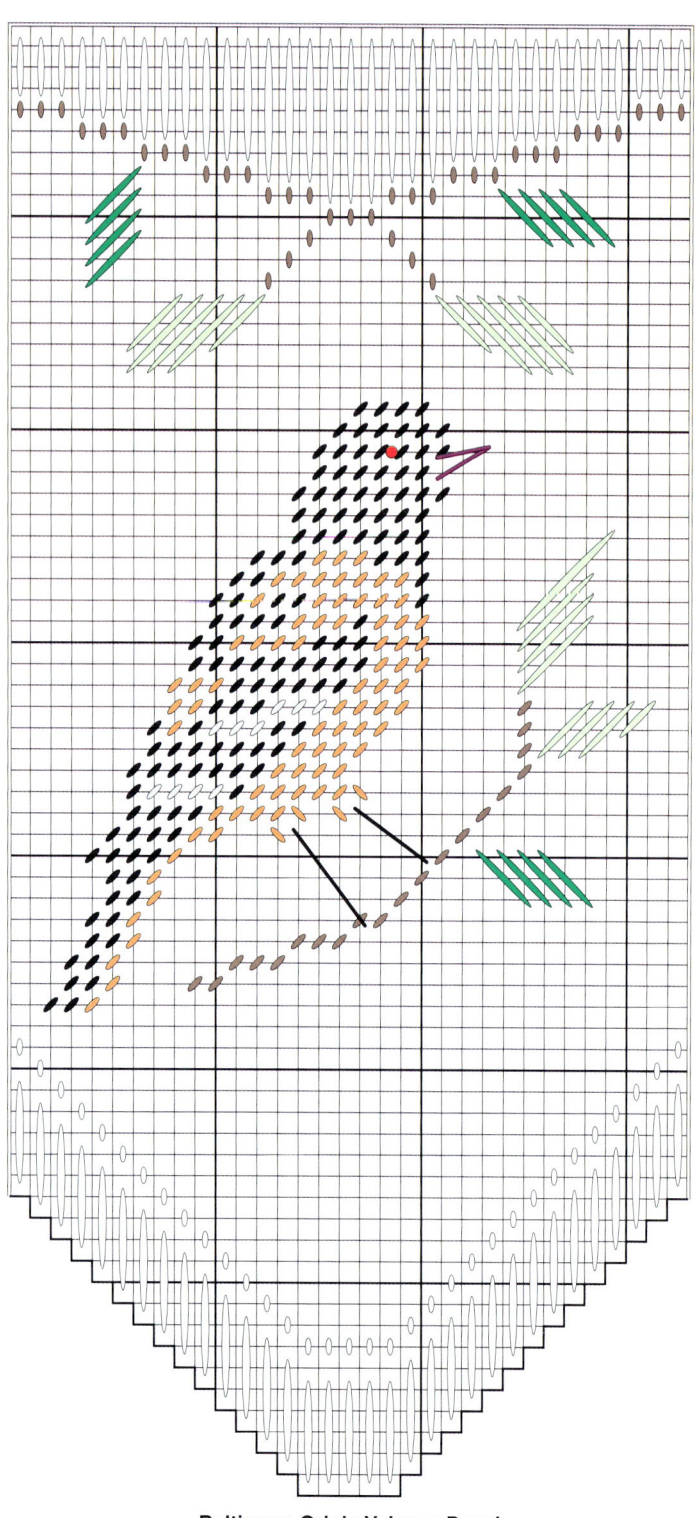

Baltimore Oriole Valance Panel
33 holes x 69 holes
Cut 3

24 Window Accents & More • The Needlecraft Shop • Berne, IN 46711 • NeedlecraftShop.com

Woodland Birds Tiebacks

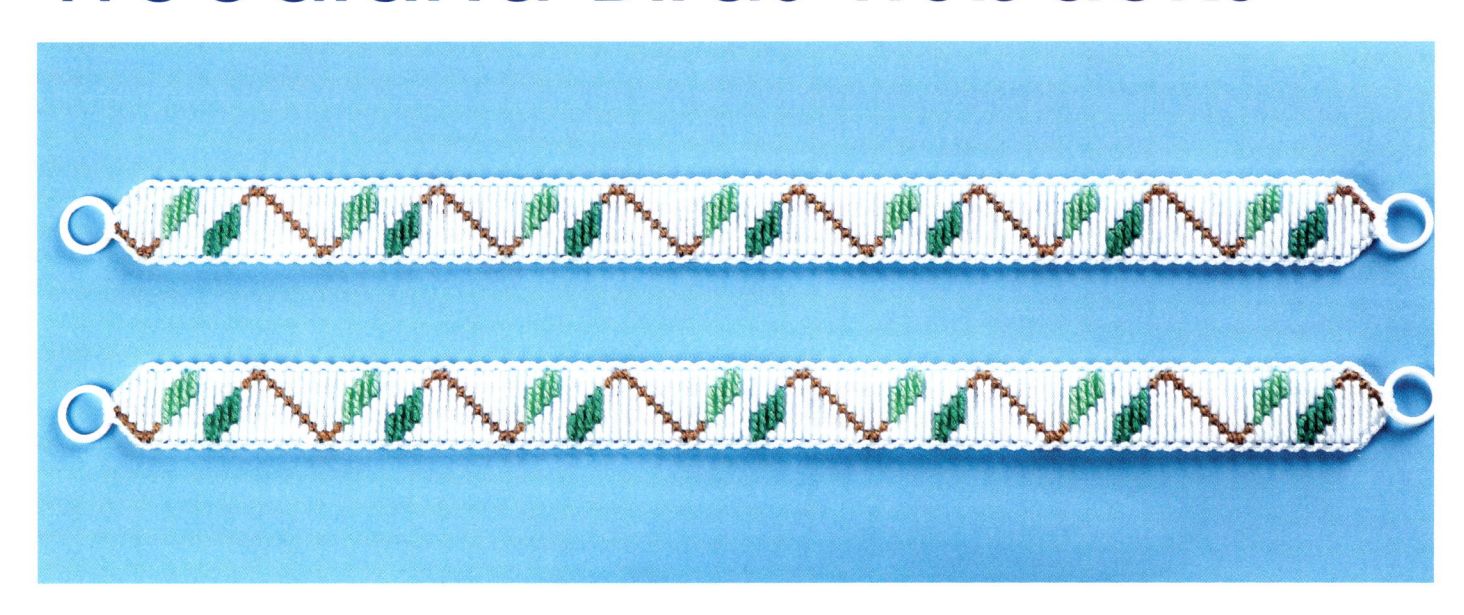

Size: 23½ inches W x 1½ inches H including white plastic rings (59.7cm x 3.8cm)
Skill Level: Beginner

Materials

- ¼ artist-size sheet 7-count plastic canvas
- Uniek Needloft plastic canvas yarn as listed in color key
- 4 (1-inch/2.5cm) white plastic rings
- #16 tapestry needle

Stitching Step by Step

1. Cut two tieback strips from plastic canvas according to graph, trimming ends identically.

2. Beginning at left end of strip, stitch each piece according to graph, continuing pattern across strip.

3. *Using white yarn throughout, Overcast edges of tieback strips:* Thread a 3-yard (2.7m) length of white yarn through center hole along one long edge; pull yarn ends even, centering yarn in hole. Working with one half of the yarn, Overcast edge, stitching through *every other hole* along straight edge and working toward end. At tapered end of strip, stitch through *every hole*, Whipstitching a plastic ring at each end as you stitch.

4. Working in the same manner, Overcast all remaining unfinished edges, attaching rings to both ends of tiebacks.

Continue pattern

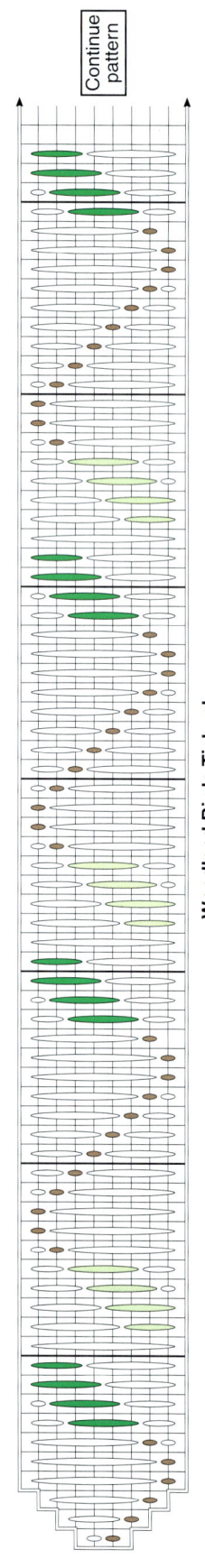

Woodland Birds Tieback
147 holes x 9 holes
Cut 2
Cut both ends identically

COLOR KEY
Yards	Plastic Canvas Yarn
4 (3.7m)	▨ Maple #13
4 (3.7m)	▢ Fern #23
4 (3.7m)	▨ Christmas green #28
23 (21m)	▢ White #41

Color numbers given are for Uniek Needloft plastic canvas yarn.

26 Window Accents & More • The Needlecraft Shop • Berne, IN 46711 • NeedlecraftShop.com

Woodland Birds Tissue Topper

Size: 4¾ inches W x 5⅝ inches H x 4¾ inches D (12.1cm x 14.3cm x 12.1cm); fits boutique-style box of tissues

Skill Level: Beginner

Materials

- ❑ 1½ sheets 7-count plastic canvas
- ❑ Uniek Needloft plastic canvas yarn as listed in color key
- ❑ Red Heart Super Saver worsted weight yarn Art. E300 as listed in color key
- ❑ Uniek Needloft metallic craft cord as listed in color key
- ❑ DMC 6-strand cotton embroidery floss as listed in color key
- ❑ 4 (8mm) round wiggly eyes
- ❑ #16 tapestry needle
- ❑ Glue

Stitching Step by Step

1 Cut two blue jay side panels, two Baltimore oriole side panels and one top from plastic canvas according to graphs.

2 Stitch sides and top according to graphs.

3 When background stitching is complete, Straight Stitch beaks using black/silver craft cord; Straight Stitch bird legs and accents on blue jay wings and tail using black yarn.

4 Using 3 strands separated from a length of very light pewter embroidery floss, work Continental Stitches over indicated stitches of white yarn along edge of blue jay's breast according to graph.

5 Glue wiggly eyes to birds where indicated by red dots on graphs.

6 Using pale yellow yarn throughout, Overcast opening in stitched top. Whipstitch side panels together along side edges, alternating blue jays and orioles, to form an open-ended square column. Whipstitch top to top edges of assembled sides. Overcast bottom edges of tissue topper.

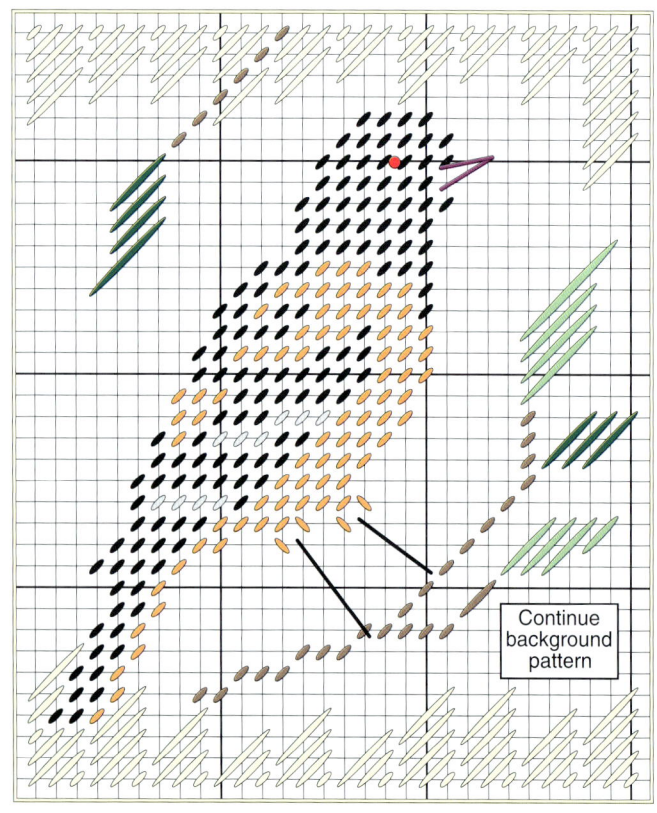

Baltimore Oriole Tissue Topper Side
31 holes x 37 holes
Cut 2

Continue background pattern

COLOR KEY

Yards	Plastic Canvas Yarn
4 (3.7m)	☐ Tangerine #11
5 (4.6m)	☐ Maple #13
4 (3.7m)	☐ Fern #23
4 (3.7m)	☐ Christmas green #28
4 (3.7m)	☐ Royal #32
1 (0.9m)	☐ Sail blue #35
1 (0.9m)	☐ Silver #37
5 (4.6m)	☐ White #41
	Worsted Weight Yarn
11 (10.1m)	■ Black #312
60 (54.9m)	☐ Pale yellow #322
	✒ Black #312 Straight Stitch
	Metallic Craft Cord
1 (0.9m)	✒ Black/silver #55010 Straight Stitch
	6-Strand Embroidery Floss
1 (0.9m)	✒ Very light pewter #168 (3 strands)
	● Attach 8mm wiggly eye

Color numbers given are for Uniek Needloft plastic canvas yarn and metallic craft cord; Red Heart Super Saver worsted weight yarn, Art. E300; and DMC 6-strand embroidery floss.

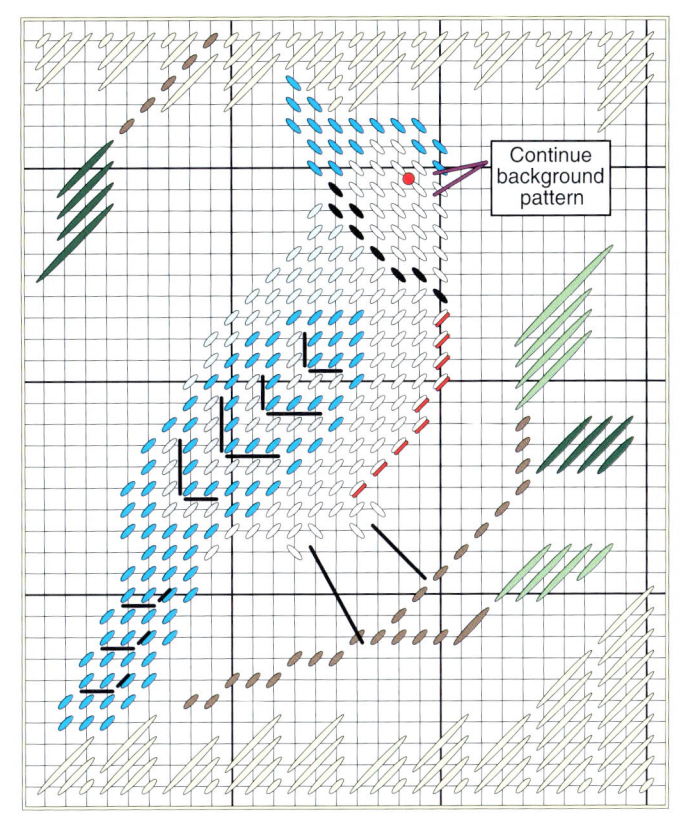

Blue Jay Tissue Topper Side
31 holes x 37 holes
Cut 2

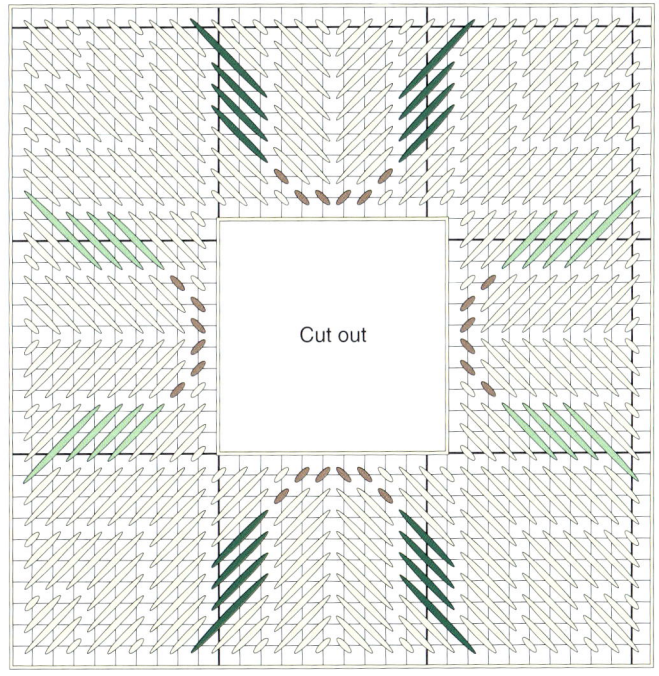

Woodland Birds Tissue Topper Top
31 holes x 31 holes
Cut 1

Woodland Birds Bookend Cover

Size: 5¼ inches W x 6⅜ inches H (13.3cm x 16.2cm); fits standard 5 x 6¼-inch (12.7cm x 15.2cm) metal bookend

Skill Level: Beginner

Materials

- 1 sheet 7-count plastic canvas
- Uniek Needloft plastic canvas yarn as listed in color key
- Worsted weight yarn as listed in color key
- Uniek Needloft metallic craft cord as listed in color key
- 8mm round wiggly eye
- 5 x 6¼-inch (12.7cm x 15.2cm) tan (or color of your choice) metal bookend
- #16 tapestry needle
- Glue

Stitching Step by Step

1 Cut two bookend cover panels from plastic canvas according to graphs.

2 Stitch one for front according to graph, filling in uncoded background with tan Continental Stitches. Second panel, for back, will remain unstitched except for Overcasting and Whipstitching.

3 When background stitching is complete, Straight Stitch beak using black/silver craft cord; Straight Stitch legs and accents on wing and tail using black yarn.

4 Glue wiggly eye to bird where indicated by red dot on graph.

5 Using tan yarn, Overcast bottom edges of stitched front and unstitched back. Hold front and back together, wrong sides facing; using maple yarn, Whipstitch front and back together up sides and over top.

6 Slide completed cover over bookend.

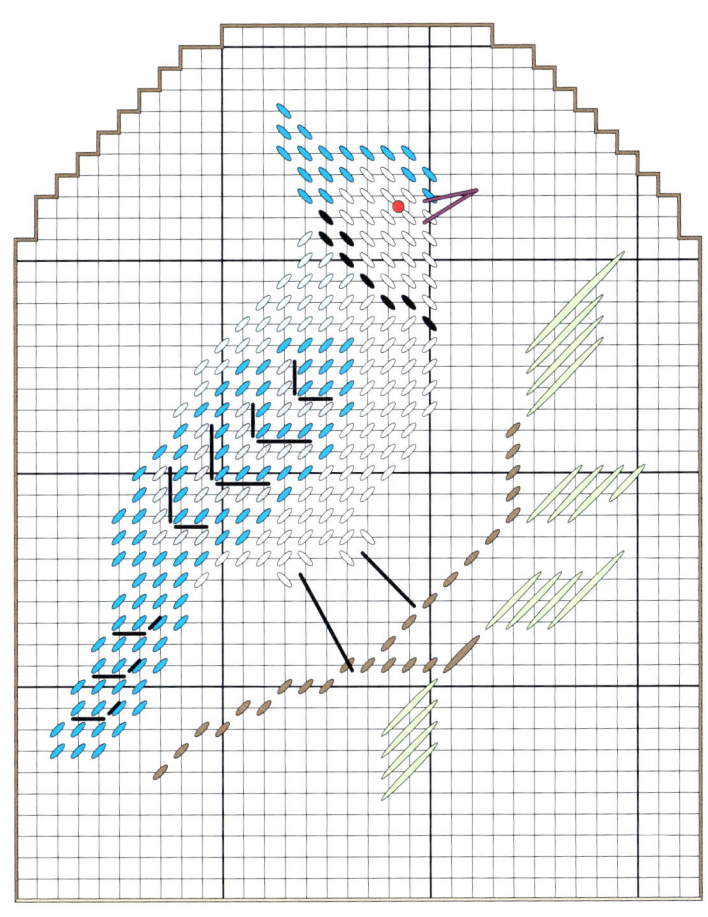

Woodland Birds Bookend Cover
33 holes x 41 holes
Cut 2, stitch 1

COLOR KEY		
Yards		**Plastic Canvas Yarn**
3 (2.7m)	■	Maple #13
2 (1.8m)	■	Royal #32
1 (0.9m)	□	Sail blue #35
1 (0.9m)	□	Silver #37
2 (1.8m)	□	White #41
2 (1.8m)	■	Bright green #61
		Worsted Weight Yarn
2 (1.8m)	■	Black #312
	/	Black #312 Straight Stitch
17 (15.5m)		Uncoded areas are tan #334 Continental Stitches
	/	Tan #334 Overcast
		Metallic Craft Cord
1 (0.9m)	/	Black/silver #55010 Straight Stitch
	●	Attach 8mm wiggly eye

Color numbers given are for Uniek Needloft plastic canvas yarn and metallic craft cord; and Red Heart Classic, Art. E267, and Super Saver, Art. E300, worsted weight yarns.

The Needlecraft Shop

306 E. Parr Road
Berne, IN 46711
NeedlecraftShop.com
© 2007 DRG. All rights reserved.

The full line of The Needlecraft Shop products is carried by Annie's Attic catalog.
TOLL-FREE ORDER LINE
or to request a free catalog
(800) 582-6643
Customer Service
(800) 449-0440
Fax (800) 882-6643
Visit AnniesAttic.com

We have made every effort to ensure the accuracy and completeness of these instructions. We cannot, however, be responsible for human error, typographical mistakes or variations in individual work. This publication may not be reproduced in part or in whole without written permission from the publisher.

ISBN: 978-1-57367-267-2
Printed in USA

1 2 3 4 5 6 7 8 9

Shopping for Supplies

For supplies, first shop your local craft and needlework stores. Some supplies may be found in fabric, hardware and discount stores. If you are unable to find the supplies you need, please call Annie's Attic at (800) 259-4000 to request a free catalog that sells plastic canvas supplies.

Getting Started

Before You Cut

Buy one brand of canvas for each entire project, as brands can differ slightly in the distance between bars. Count holes carefully from the graph before you cut, using the bolder lines that show each 10 holes. These 10-mesh lines begin in the lower left corner of each graph to make counting easier. Mark canvas before cutting, then remove all marks completely before stitching. If the piece is cut in a rectangular or square shape and is either not worked, or worked with only one color and one type of stitch, we do not include the graph in the pattern. Instead, we give the cutting and stitching instructions in the general instructions or with the individual project instructions.

Covering the Canvas

Bring needle up from back of work, leaving a short length of yarn on back of canvas; work over short length to secure. To end a thread, weave needle and thread through the wrong side of your last few stitches; clip. Follow the numbers on the small graphs beside each stitch illustration; bring your needle up from the back of the work on odd numbers and down through the front of the work on even numbers. Work embroidery stitches last, after the canvas has been completely covered by the needlepoint stitches.

Basic Stitches

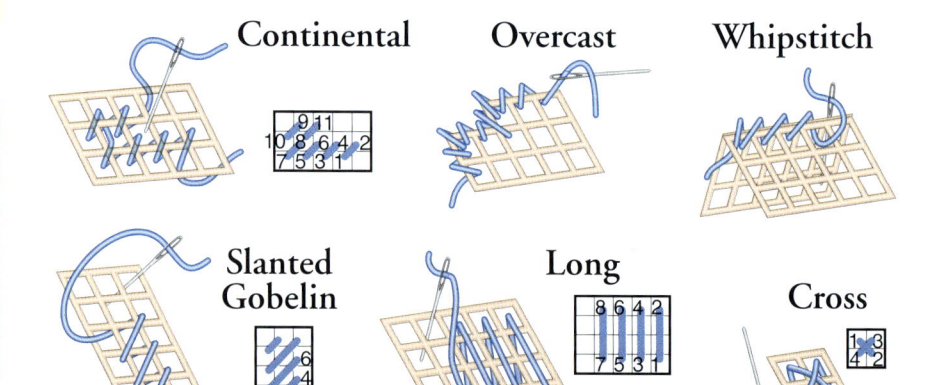

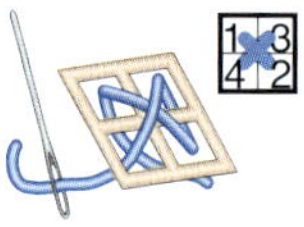

Continental
Overcast
Whipstitch
Slanted Gobelin
Long
Cross

Embroidery Stitches

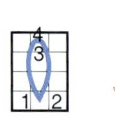

French Knot 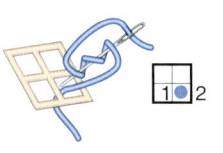
Lazy Daisy 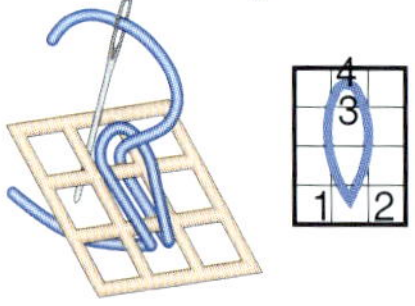
Backstitch 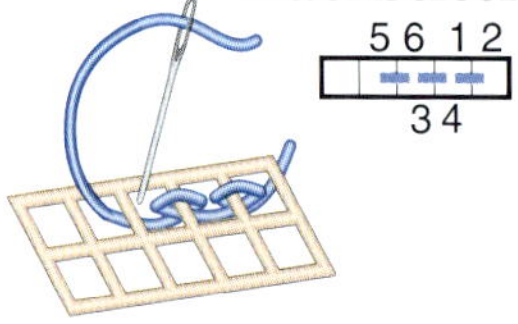
Straight

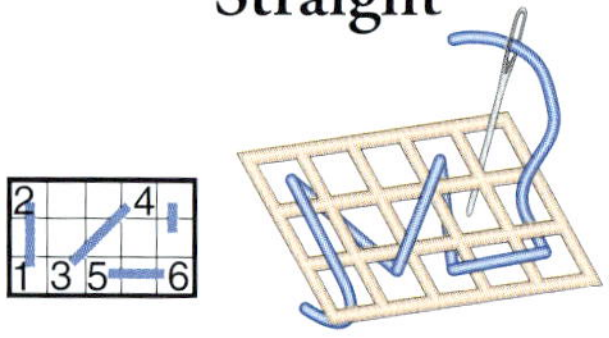

METRIC KEY:
millimeters = (mm)
centimeters = (cm)
meters = (m)
grams = (g)